SCRIMSHAW

A COMPLETE ILLUSTRATED MANUAL

by Steve Paszkiewicz
and Roger Schroeder

SECOND EDITION

Fox Chapel Publishing

1970 Broad Street • East Petersburg, PA 17520
www.FoxChapelPublishing.com

Dedication

Dedicated to our wives, Ellie and Sheila, for their continued love and support.

Acknowledgements

We wish to thank William Gilkerson for allowing us to create artwork based on his original scrimshaw that appeared in his book *The Scrimshander*. And we thank Sheila Schroeder for her expert proofreading of the manuscript.

Alan Giagnocavo
Publisher

Gretchen Bacon
Assistant Book Editor

Ayleen Stellhorn
Project Editor

Kerri Landis
Editorial Assistant

Troy Thorne
Creative Direction

Linda L. Eberly
Layout Design

Roger Schroeder
Interior Photography

Jon Deck
Cover Design

ISBN 1–56523–241–0

Library of Congress Cataloging-in-Publication Data

Paszkiewicz, Steve.

    Scrimshaw : a complete illustrated manual / by Steve Paszkiewicz and Roger Schroeder. -- 2nd ed. -- East Petersburg, PA : Fox Chapel Publishing, c2005.

        p. ; cm.
        Includes bibliographical references.
        ISBN: 1-56523-241-0

        1. Scrimshaws. 2. Ivory carving. 3. Carving (Decorative arts)
I. Schroeder, Roger. II. Title.

TT288 .P37 2005
736/.69--dc22   0501

To learn more about the other great books
from Fox Chapel Publishing, or to find a
retailer near you, call toll-free 1-800-457-9112
or visit us at **www.FoxChapelPublishing.com.**

Printed in China
10 9 8 7 6 5 4 3 2 1

Table of Contents

Steve Paszkiewicz

Although Steve Paszkiewicz considers himself a landlubber, he has spent nearly half his life involved with nautical art. Since 1971 he has been constructing award-winning model ship replicas with the finest details.

As a young man, he spent a decade as a diamond prospector in South America. After returning to the United States, he worked as a silk screen photographer.

With a degree from art school, Steve tried out a variety of art mediums, from painting to woodcarving. He hit upon scrimshaw when he met a man etching pictures on beef bone. Steve took a liking to scrimshaw and quickly graduated from bone to ivory. He has spent over two decades as a scrimshander, the term used to describe an engraver of bone, ivory and other organic materials.

Steve lives with his wife, Ellie, in Whitestone, New York.

Roger Schroeder

Roger Schroeder's success as a writer began when he gave up trying to write the great American novel. Instead, he turned to writing about his hobby: woodworking. Sharpening his skills and his photography and expanding his interests, he went on to author 15 books and over 200 magazine articles. Ranging in scope from woodcarving to housebuilding, the books include titles such as *How to Carve Wildfowl, Carving Signs, Making Toys* and *Timber Frame Construction*. He is also the founding editor of *Wood Carving Illustrated* magazine.

Roger enjoys lecturing on topics such as how to make wood into furniture, houses and sculpture. In the remaining time he is an amateur cabinetmaker—specializing in Victorian reproductions—and an amateur bird carver who has received a number of blue ribbons for his natural wood sculptures.

Roger lives with his wife, Sheila, in Amityville, Long Island, New York.

Scrimshaw is considered by many to be one of the original American art forms, having gained popularity in the 1800s among sailors, especially those on whaling ships. Because whale teeth and bone had little commercial value, these materials were readily available to sailors for scrimshaw. Many of the scrimshaw pieces of the 1800s were unschooled renderings on implements often of a practical nature. As the whaling industry declined, so did the practice of scrimshaw. However, in the mid-1900s, scrimshaw started to regain popularity. This resurgence is sometimes attributed to President John F. Kennedy, an avid scrimshaw collector who often displayed pieces from his collection in the White House. As an awareness of the art form grew, so did the number of scrimshanders. Today, there are many master scrimshaw artists who practice a variety of techniques. Instead of the typical black ink on a white surface, some scrimshaw work is done on dark material with white or colored ink. Finding that the original materials—whale teeth and bone and elephant ivory—were scarce or would further endanger wildlife, modern scrimshanders have turned to alternative materials for scrimshaw. Fossilized ivory, vegetable ivory, shed antler, and polymers are just some of the materials used today.

The art of scrimshaw is a tactile affair for both the artist and the collector. Too often, art seems intimidating, and being able to handle a piece of scrimshaw, to study the depth of each incision and note the infinite stippling, is an intimate and gratifying experience. There are some who would still consider scrimshaw only a folk art, usually because of the unschooled qualities of early pieces. However, there are many artists today whose efforts I prefer to describe as fine art on an alternate canvas.

One does not have to be an artist to practice the art of scrimshaw. The archaic and natural character of bone, ivory, or shell lends itself to creative endeavor, and I encourage the reader to discover his or her innate talent.

Fair Winds,
Holly Hawkins
Gallery Director

The Maritime Gallery at Mystic Seaport
The Museum of America and the Sea
PO Box 6000
47 Greenmanville Avenue
Mystic, CT 06355
(860) 572-5388
Fax: (860) 572-5324
gallery@mysticseaport.org
www.mysticseaport.org/gallery

About Mystic Seaport and the Maritime Gallery

Founded in 1929, Mystic Seaport is now our country's leading maritime museum, guardian of the largest collections of scrimshaw, boats, and sea-related photography in the world. This private not-for-profit educational institution annually serves over a million visitors from around the globe, approximately 25,000 members from each of the 50 states and 30 foreign countries, and boasts a volunteer corps of over 700 dedicated individuals who believe in the power of the American maritime experience that connects us all. For more information about the museum and its operations, please call the Mystic Seaport Information Line at (860) 572-5315 or toll free at **1-888-9SEAPORT** (1-888-973-2767).

The Maritime Gallery at Mystic Seaport is the nation's foremost gallery specializing in contemporary marine art and ship models. Founded in 1979, it has become the recognized leader in the field. Working closely with the world's finest marine artists, the gallery is in a unique position to offer collectors their choice from among the best work on the market. In addition to hosting major theme exhibitions each year, the gallery always has on hand hundreds of paintings, ship models, sculptures, and scrimshaw on nearly every subject relating to the sea. As varied as these works are, they all have one thing in common—they are among the finest examples of their kind available anywhere.

I magine you are a sailor in the middle of the 19th century, put aboard a ship that leaves from New Bedford, Massachusetts, Sag Harbor, New York, or one of several other ports. You are with some 30 other sailors set out to hunt and kill an aquatic mammal many tons in weight. The animal you pursue, the whale, will not be turned into food. Rather, you hunt it for materials far more precious: oil and baleen, a stiff, leathery material taken from a whale's mouth. Back home the light that illuminates your home has its source in the oil you return with; the girl left in port wears a corset made in part from baleen, 19th century's "plastic."

Unfortunately, life aboard the ship is rarely a happy one. You face mean-spirited supervisors, filth, scurvy, poor food, fights, and even floggings. In the tropics you swelter, off Antarctica you freeze. You receive a "lay" or share in the profits, but necessities are charged to your account; you may return to port in debt. And you could be as many as five years at sea!

The dangers on the ocean are many, not the least of which are storms, but whale hunting is especially dangerous. Simply put, the whale does not take kindly to being harpooned. An angry whale can use its flukes to shatter a boat and drown the men aboard.

Perhaps ironically, tedium is also an enemy. To hunt the whale, it is necessary to have a larger crew than is needed to run the ship. Much of your time, then, is unproductive. But, there is a ray of hope if you are inclined to use your hands. Whale teeth and whale bone have little commercial value. After the blubber is stripped from the whale, these discards are available. Given nothing more than a knife and a few dental-looking tools, you are on your way to creating a piece of scrimshaw art from tooth and bone.

Scrimshaw, with its engravings of nautical themes, patriotic motifs, elegant ladies and sometimes erotic art, comes from the early part of the 19th century. It is believed that Americans learned about carving and engraving ivory during the War of 1812, possibly on British prison ships. After the war, which freed America from British tyranny at sea, long voyages to seas as far away as the Indian Ocean became possible. Since such a trip could take several years, the vacuum of inactivity had to be filled. And so, an old art form was adapted and made into an American folk art.

What is the origin of the word scrimshaw? The very comprehensive *Oxford English Dictionary* (which almost always has the last word in etymology) indicates that the origin of the word is obscure, although it may have been influenced by an older word, scrimshank, which means to shirk or ignore one's duties. A captain out of New Bedford, Massachusetts wrote in his logbook of 1836: "An idle head is the workshop of the devil. Employed scrimshon."

An often quoted passage from Herman Melville's *Moby Dick* reads that whalemen "have little boxes of dentistical-looking implements, specially intended for the skrimshandering business. But, in general, they toil with their jackknives alone; and, with that almost omnipotent tool of the sailor, they will turn out anything you please, in the way of a mariner's fancy."

Engraved scrimshaw for the whaler usually meant the tooth of the sperm whale; yet whale bone, walrus tusks, porpoise jaws, and even baleen were all engraved and often carved to create intricate fans, jewelry, cane heads, knitting and embroidery items, and pieces for inlay work. A form of ivory, the teeth of the lower jaw of the sperm whale can number 50 and measure up to 10 inches in length. However, a tooth could not be worked on in its natural state. Having ridges, it is not at all smooth. So the scrimshander had to prepare it. He first soaked it in brine, or hot water and lye, to keep it soft since it hardened when exposed to air. He next filed it and then smoothed it with sharkskin, a natural "sandpaper." The tooth was ready for engraving.

The sailor simply sketched a picture on the tooth with a pencil, or he traced it, following the outline made by a series of dots done with a pointed instrument. His sources of inspiration were the ship he was on, the hunted whales, or a magazine or illustrated book from home. The drawing was engraved using a pointed piece of steel or sharp knife. The next step was filling in the lines; sailors used ink, tar, paint, lampblack—even tobacco juice. Finally he polished it with pumice or sailmaker's wax to give it a sheen.

Art work involving ivory was not confined to whale's teeth and bone. Elephant ivory was available in the ancient worlds of Greece, Rome, and Egypt. Using ivory as an art medium was popular in the Orient for nearly a millennium.

Elephant ivory was put to different uses as the 19th century turned into the 20th. Billiard balls were needed to meet a growing interest in the game; piano keys required a hard, white shiny surface. Ivory was the perfect material for both. Great Britain was a major source of piano keys and billiards balls. In 1890, for instance, nearly a million and a half pounds of elephant ivory were imported to that country. It took approximately 50,000 elephants to produce that much.

It was inevitable that society's needs and interests would change. The elephant population was diminished and a substitute had to be found. It was plastic, which is now used for billiard balls and piano keys. As for the whale, the discovery of petroleum made whale oil too expensive to obtain, and plastics replaced baleen. When the last United States whaling ship set sail from Massachusetts in 1924 and sank, the American whaling industry was over.

People paid little attention to scrimshaw until the 1960s. Aside from a few serious collectors, the public on the whole was unaware of the history of scrimshaw. It was the late President John F. Kennedy who took an interest in it—he was from Massachusetts and spent time on the islands that were once whaling ports—and he even displayed pieces on his presidential desk. More than 30 years later, genuine scrimshaw in the form of teeth or whale bone is highly collectible, though extremely scarce.

Today, as the art form is being revived by scrimshanders like Walter Alexander, Kristin Barndt, Sandra Brady, Deb Donnelly, William Gilkerson, Bob Hergert, Anouk Johanna, Catherine Nerbonne, Viveca Sahlin, Kurt Sperry, Mark Thogerson and Robert Weiss. Many materials besides ivory offer good possibilities for scrimshaw work. There are naturally shed antlers, tougher than ivory; the material is ideal for a variety of accessories such as knife handles. Walrus ivory is also available if legally obtained from Eskimos. Mammoth and mastodon ivory, when found, is another medium for scrimshaw, but minerals may have replaced some of the ivory.

Tagua nut, or "vegetable ivory," is a renewable source of scrimshanding material. Old piano keys offer small but useful pieces for diminutive work.

Many other materials offer surfaces for scrimshaw. A shell, provided it has a smooth surface to work on, can be engraved. Even beef bone, available from butchers and slaughterhouses, makes an interesting medium for scrimshaw.

Possibly the most commonly used material today for scrimshaw is the very material that saved the elephant from total extinction. Polymer plastic being a polymeric substance is made to look so much like ivory that it is very difficult to detect the substitution.

Scrimshaw shows you what you need to get started in the art form. Ivory-like materials are available that endanger no species. Tools are easily purchased from an art supply store or a good home center. You learn how to prepare your medium, even cut it if necessary. And you get instruction in engraving, a technique you may be doing for the first time.

Tips on transferring patterns are offered. How do you take a picture from a book or magazine and put it on an irregularly shaped object?

Solutions are given. Looking for a pattern? Try clipart books, clipart from CD-Roms or one of the patterns offered in the book. And be advised that you are not limited to nautical themes. Many scrimshanders today are creating beautiful work on objects such as knife handles using American game and African animals as subjects.

Read the chapter on shading and coloring if you want to know how to turn your scrimshaw into a colorful work of art.

Have you come across a piece of scrimshaw and want to know whether it is a genuine 19th-century piece or a late 20th-century reproduction? Tips on how to tell the real from the fake are outlined in Chapter Six.

In search of inspiration? Look through the gallery of finished pieces.

The book brings you to a project of a sailing ship. From pattern to finished work, you learn step by step the simple techniques of scrimshanding.

Scrimshaw closes with a list of tool suppliers, sources for alternative ivory and books on the history of the art form.

Happy scrimshanding.

Gallery

STEVE PASZKIEWICZ

On the pages of this gallery section, you will find, first, a collection of scrimshaw pieces from Steve Paszkiewicz and, second, scrimshaw pieces from other scrimshaw artists. Provided for each artist is a short biography with some information about their style of scrimshaw and a few examples of their work. The gallery certainly does not include a complete list of the outstanding scrimshaw artists who are scrimshanding today; rather it provides a sampling of those artists. Browse through the section and use it to help get your creative juices flowing.

Steve Paszkiewicz is an artist who works in a variety of art forms, and he especially enjoys scrimshaw. Much of his scrimshaw work is done in the style of the 19th-century sailors and focuses on nautical themes. Steve works with needles, diamond tools, and whatever else it takes to create a work of art.

Depiction of a whale breaking water after diving. Mammoth elephant ivory.

The Victory, Admiral Nelson's flagship. Beef bone.

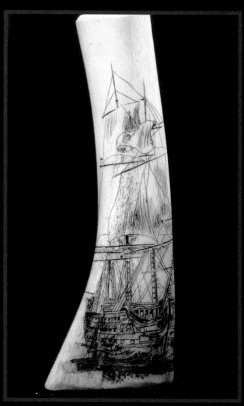

Another view of The Victory. Beef bone.

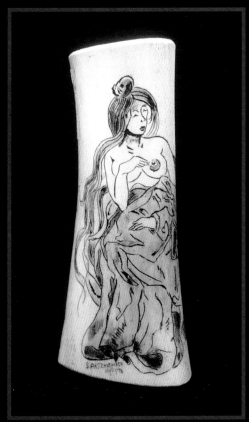

Geisha girl. Beef bone.

Wavertree. Beef bone.

Hairbrush with traditional eagle design. Elephant ivory.

Another hairbrush with eagle design. Elephant ivory.

Gallery

STEVE PASZKIEWICZ

Powder container with the clipper ship *Flying Cloud*.
Elephant ivory.

Piano key with lighthouse. Elephant ivory.

Polychrome sailing ship. Elephant ivory.

Maiden on dolphin. Based on an original scrimshaw
design by William Gilkerson. Elephant ivory.

STEVE PASZKIEWICZ

A whaling scene. Elephant ivory.

The bark *Charles W. Morgan*, America's most famous whaler, on cigarette case. Based on an original scrimshaw design by William Gilkerson. Elephant ivory.

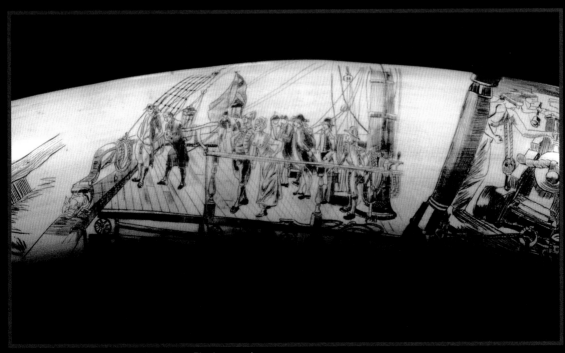

Admiral Nelson meets Lady Hamilton. Elephant tusk.

STEVE PASZKIEWICZ

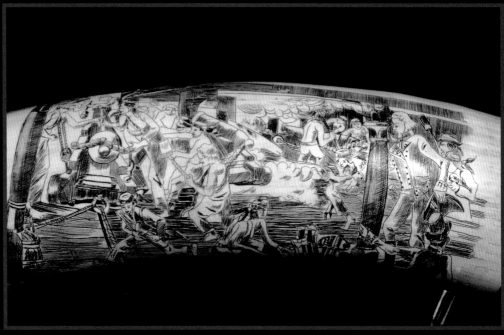

Interior of warship. Men firing cannons. Elephant tusk.

The brig *Pilgrim*. Based on an original scrimshaw design by William Gilkerson. Elephant ivory.

Another view of the *Pilgrim*. Based on an original scrimshaw design by William Gilkerson. Elephant ivory.

The *U.S.S. Constitution*. Beef bone.

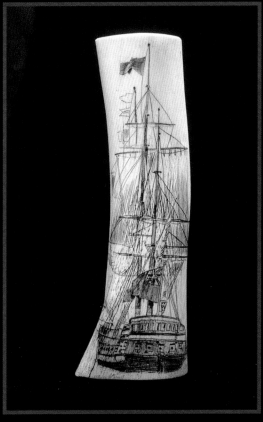

The Victory. Polychrome stern view. Beef bone.

Cannon and powder monkey on powder box.
Elephant ivory.

Gun crew and cannon on powder box. Based on
an original scrimshaw design by William
Gilkerson. Elephant ivory.

STEVE PASZKIEWICZ

Battle between American and English frigates. Polymer.

Billiard ball with map of the world. Elephant ivory.

Another view of billiard ball world map.

STEVE PASZKIEWICZ

The ship *Vicar of Bray* in harbor. Elephant ivory.

Flying Cloud on a bolo. Slabbed billiard ball. Elephant ivory.

Charles W. Morgan on pendant. Slabbed billiard ball. Elephant ivory.

STEVE PASZKIEWICZ

Whaling ship.

U.S.S. Constitution on pendant. Slabbed billiard ball. Elephant ivory.

Whaling ship. Whale tooth.

Kristen Barndt has been winning awards for her drawings since the age of seven, so it was natural that she study art in college and begin a graphic design studio with her husband after graduation. "I've loved animals, especially horses and wildlife, since childhood," she says, "and they are among my favorite art subjects." Her artistic nature, combined with encouragement from her knife-collecting husband, drew her toward scrimshaw. She specializes in "reverse" scrimshaw. "I use a darker-colored material and scrim only the light areas of the design, allowing the dark material to define shadows and other dark areas," she explains. Kristen's materials include black water buffalo horn, jet stone, black paper Micarta, dark brown mastodon or mammoth ivory, and pipe stone. After polishing the material to a mirror gloss, she stipples or scratches the design, then coats it with white paint, which contrasts with the dark background. "Color can also be used in the reverse technique," she notes, "but the application is more difficult than in traditional scrimshaw."

The Balance of Life (Wolf and Caribou), each 1⅜" wide x 3½" high, reverse scrimshaw technique on black paper Micarta pistol grips.

Puffins, 5" long x 1½" high, reverse scrimshaw technique with spot color on genuine black water buffalo horn.

Grand Slam Rams (Bighorn Sheep, Dall Sheep, Desert Sheep, Stone Sheep), approximately 3⅜" long x ⅞" high, traditional scrimshaw on genuine ivory knife handles.

Featured Artists

DEB DONNELLY

In 1996, **Deb Donnelly** got a job as a scrimshander—then went to the library to learn how to do it. An artist in a variety of mediums, including pencil and watercolors, Deb owned a small scrimshawed necklace but had never tried the technique. "It was an intriguing new challenge," she says. After learning about tools and materials, Deb practiced on acrylic, bone, antler, tusks, nuts, and Corian before working up to real ivory. To incise her designs, she has used everything from a sewing needle to a drill bit blank to an electric scrimshaw machine; she prefers to work by hand, aided by a magnifying lens or microscope for the fine, stippled details. She creates both her own and custom designs. "Scrimshaw is almost a lost art," she says. "It's very satisfying."

Woman's face piano key, ivory.

Wolf necklace, 1½"; earrings, ½", Corian.

Indian girl belt buckle, 3", ivory.

Cowboy pistol grip, Micarta.

BOB HERGERT

Bob Hergert has always "sensed that art was the inevitable path [he] must follow." Toward that end, he worked as a technical illustrator, painted murals, sold original drawings—and drove a school bus during his leaner times. In 1978, a jeweler friend suggested he try scrimshaw, gave him ivory cabochons to scratch, and introduced him to an ivory dealer. One introduction led to another, and soon Bob was specializing in micro-scrimshaw on miniature knife handles.

A full-time scrimshander now, Bob stipples with a carbide tool "so fine it can cut a point as small as a dust particle!" He works mainly on fossil ivory and fills his designs with black oil paint in the traditional method, though his subjects (which range from wildlife to motorcycles, buildings, and monuments) are far from standard. He has also scrimmed some unusual objects, including guitar knobs and accents, mother-of-pearl pens, and Zippo lighters. Interestingly, Bob was featured as a character in Tom Clancy's novel *Net Force: Point of Impact.* "Although my part was small, I was significant to the plot," he says. And the mention might be good for the art of scrimshaw. "I am an avid promoter of scrimshaw and work to educate the general public about the timeless quality of the art."

Samuel American Horse strikes a noble pose on a David Boye folder, 3½". Fossil ivory scales.

Cossacks, 3" × 5". Fossil mammoth ivory.

Big Ben, Ancora fountain pen, mother of pearl.

One of a set of four lizards, 3" × 5". Wooly mammoth ivory.

Featured Artists

ANOUK JOHANNA

Anouk Johanna is a versatile artist who works in a variety of media, including pen and ink, watercolors, prints, and jewelry design. She specializes in scrimming teddy bears, dolls, storybook characters, and pets on handmade jewelry. "I discovered teddy bear, doll, and collectible shows 20 years ago," she says. "They inspired me....The subject matter allows me to tune in to the whimsical aspect of scrimshaw, and I have always enjoyed that." In fact, Anouk enjoys the whimsical so much that she does not do more traditional scrimshaw themes like seascapes or wildlife.

Anouk uses cross-hatching to create her designs. "I personally like to see engraved lines in scrimshaw," she says. However, her customers don't always understand what they're seeing. "People can hardly believe I actually hand-engrave every little line white on white and then paint so these lines become visible," she says with a laugh. "I have had people ask me more than once if it was a decal on plastic or if it was a photo-transfer!"

Two brothers, 1¼" x ¾"; teardrop dangle earrings with hand-engraved and painted images. 14/20 Goldfill earwires.

Louisa, 1¾" x 1¼"; brooch with hand-engraved and painted image on Siberian fossil mammoth ivory. Inlaid in 14/20 Goldfill and cocobolo wood.

Buster, 4½"; hand-engraved and painted image on Siberian fossil mammoth ivory.

Hecate, 2⅛" x 1⅜"; brooch with hand-engraved and painted image on Siberian fossil mammoth ivory. Inlaid in 14/20 Goldfill and ebony wood.

CATHERINE NERBONNE

According to **Catherine Nerbonne's** baby book, her favorite things to do as a child were going to the zoo and drawing with crayons. It was almost inevitable that she would become an artist, biologist, and scientific illustrator, and scrimshaw follows naturally from those interests. Catherine met Mark while she was a student. "He said, 'You can do this,' gave me one lesson, and I've been doing it ever since," she remembers. Her primary inspiration comes from the natural world, and she often visits zoos, parks, and museums with her sketchbook or a camera in hand. She enjoys doing scrimshaw on naturally-shed antler and fossil ivory, but has etched on materials as diverse as recycled slate shingles, elk antlers, and pool cues. "People in different places in the country want different things from their scrimshaw," she observes. "Different themes, different materials. It keeps the work interesting."

Wolf and tiger pendants set in sterling; tiger 1½" x 2"; mammoth ivory.

Pool cue inlay; ⅞"; mammoth ivory set in turquoise and exotic woods.

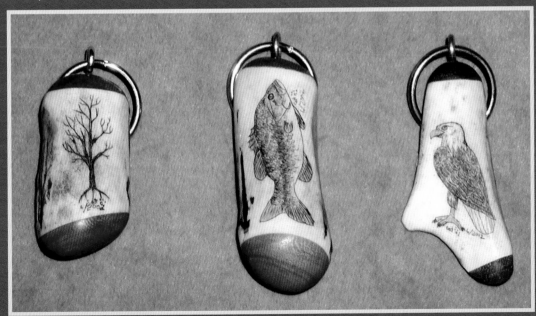

Keyrings; 2" diameter; whitetail deer antler.

Featured Artists

VIVECA SAHLIN

Viveca Sahlin started doing scrimshaw in 1995, learning it the hard way—by trial and error. She likes the challenge of creating small details in her scrimshaw art but sometimes finds it frustrating, too. "It is very time-consuming," she admits. Her only tools are a pin vise and needles, and she mainly uses a stippling technique. While Viveca often bases her designs on photos, she draws them freehand, usually starting with the eyes and working out. She is particularly well known for her wildlife and fantasy themes and incises many of them on knife handles. In addition to scrimshaw, Viveca dabbles in oil painting and pencil drawings.

Dragon knife

Magician

Tiger

Two wolves

Kurt Sperry began scrimshawing in 1976 when a fellow high school student introduced him to the medium. "I loved it," he says. "I was immediately drawn to the fine detail it was possible to render in the medium as well as the fascinating material—mammoth ivory—upon which the work was done." Kurt honed his craft working at the Alaska Scrimshaw & Ivory Company in Bellingham, Washington, for four years, learning more advanced techniques such as stippling and the use of color or polychrome. He discovered globes about 15 years ago after seeing one a friend found in London. He draws the designs freehand, inspired mainly by 17th-century Dutch maps. "They are the apogee of elaborate cartography," he says. "They are the most popular because they're quite ornate, have cute errors, and are colorful." While it's difficult to procure the old ivory billiard balls because manufacturers stopped making them in the 1930s, they are one of his favorite materials. "The balls tend to be cracked, which is annoying to work on, but the imperfections give the globes a wonderful patina." Kurt's globes span the cartographic period from the late 15th century to the modern day. The globes inspired by ornate 17th-century Dutch maps are his most popular style.

Untitled, based on a 17th-century Dutch world map, 2½". Antique ivory billiard ball, rosewood stand with mammoth ivory inlays.

Globe featuring the clipper ship *Westward Ho*, 2". Antique ivory billiard ball, rosewood stand.

MARK THOGERSON

Mark Thogerson taught himself scrimshaw at age 13 after seeing a sample in a shop and thinking, "I could do that." He used his allowance to buy whale's teeth, found some books, and started practicing. He has developed many of his own techniques over his 30-year tenure as a scrimshander but has tried to stay true to the origins of the craft by using simple tools—specifically, a metal scribe—and natural materials. His favorite subjects are nautical and nature, especially wildflower, themes. He has been exhibiting his work at art fairs since 1975. He has been a naturalist, a park ranger, a database analyst, and a "professional student." He is currently an adjunct professor in biology and works for a regional land trust as a field ecologist.

Ruffed grouse cribbage board detail; design 2½" long; elk antler using brown ink.

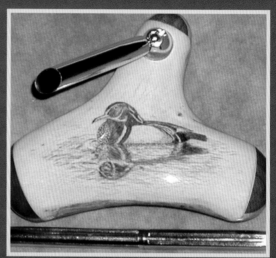

Pen set; pen is approximately 6" long; mule deer antler.

Bookmarks; ½" × 4"; piano key ivory; eighth note is pierced, not scrimmed.

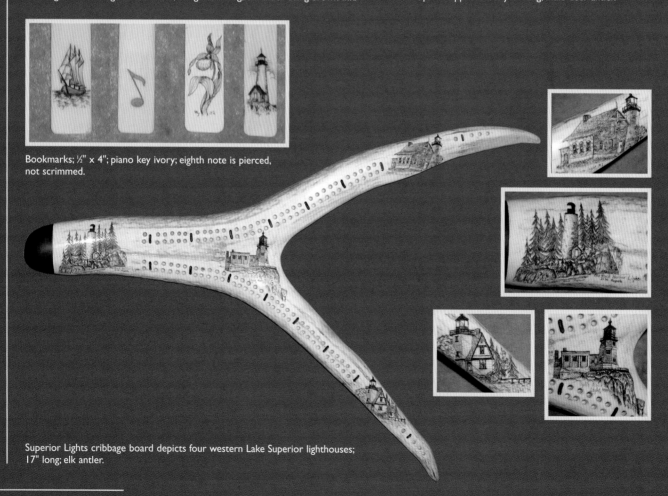

Superior Lights cribbage board depicts four western Lake Superior lighthouses; 17" long; elk antler.

A variety of materials is available to you for scrimshaw. Some are readily accessible—polymer, for example—and others are as scarce as whale's teeth.

THE WHALE TOOTH AND OTHER IVORIES

The Marine Mammal Protection and Endangered Species Acts restricted whale ivory to such an extent that only teeth that entered the United States before 1973 and sold by a dealer licensed from the Fish and Wildlife Service can be purchased. Despite these stringent restrictions, the sperm whale tooth makes an ideal medium for scrimshaw.

Fossil ivory is another source for scrimshaw. Woolly mastodons and mammoths last roamed the world ten thousand years ago. If their tusks survived the millennia, they are usually found in such exotic places as Siberia. They are difficult to work and costly to purchase.

A whale's tooth is a hard and dense material. Elephant ivory is softer than whale ivory. It also has a grain that looks almost like a dense wood grain with interlocking lines. Fortunately for the animal, importing elephant ivory into the United States has stopped altogether. However, in 1997 a United Nations wildlife organization downgraded the protected status of elephants in three African nations, allowing limited international trade. What this means for the fate of the African elephant is unclear, but it is hoped that artists will search out alternatives to elephant ivory. If it is necessary to use the material, there are sources for small pieces of ivory available before the import ban (see Sources for Supplies in the back of this book). When large pieces of elephant ivory or tusks are obtained—presumably from animals that died of natural causes—they are usually slabbed into thin pieces to avoid waste. This organic material is expensive, with a single tusk costing thousands of dollars.

Piano keys were made from elephant ivory until the 1930s. Search out the yellow pages for piano restorers, especially ones working on antique player pianos. Large antique shows may be another source.

While the typical piano key is small, measuring about $\frac{1}{16}$" thick and less than 1 inch wide, the key does make for a scrimshaw medium. In fact, with careful gluing—use an epoxy glue—keys can be joined together to create a larger surface.

Still another source of ivory is an antique billiard ball. At one time made from elephant ivory, the ball, about 2" in diameter, offers a perfectly round object to work on when it is cut into thin pieces. Billiard ball sections, even ones made of polymer, can be engraved and turned into bolos, pendants or cameos.

A sperm whale tooth engraved by Steve Paszkiewicz.

Piano keys make for small pieces of scrimshaw.

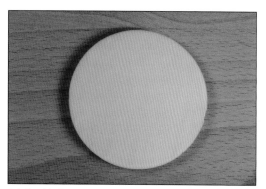

A billiard ball, even one made of plastic as pictured, can be slabbed and the resulting section engraved.

Shells can be scrimshawed, but the outer surface may be too difficult to smooth. The inside of this shell is suitable for engraving.

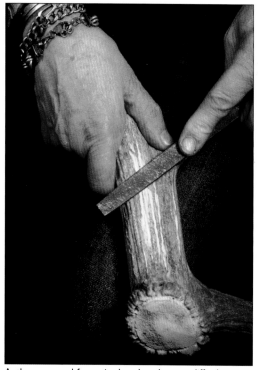

Antlers are used for scrimshaw, but they are difficult to work with hand tools. Power grinding is better.

The outer surface of a nautilus shell is an ideal surface for scrimshaw.

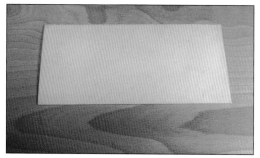

Polymer ivory comes in thin sheets that need no surface preparation before engraving.

ANTLERS AND HORNS

Moose, elk, deer and caribou all have antlers. The material is very hard, but it can be filed and polished. Machine grinding and polishing may be necessary. Once it is smooth, an antler or a piece of one makes an excellent medium for scrimshaw.

Steers offer horns as an art medium. Available in the Southwest, their surfaces can be scrimshawed without having to change their interesting shapes.

SHELLS

The smooth interior of a shell, which is as hard as it feels, can be engraved. Some shells—a nautilus is an example—have smooth exteriors which can be engraved easily. Shells that have rough exteriors require a lot of filing to get them smooth and may not be suitable for most people looking for a scrimshaw medium.

The tagua nut has been used as an ivory substitute for over a century.

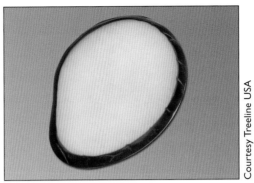

When slabbed, the nut produces small pieces for scrimshaw.

Courtesy Treeline USA

A problem with tagua nuts is that they usually contain cavities that cannot be seen on the surface.

POLYMER IVORY

Because of our concern for endangered species such as whales and elephants, polymer—or polyester ivory as it is sometimes called—has become the popular substitute for many scrimshanders. Having the look and feel of real ivory, and relatively inexpensive, it can be purchased in thin sheets (see Sources for Supplies). A sheet measuring 4" by 5" will probably cost under 20 dollars. Some manufacturers claim that age can be simulated by soaking the polymer in tea—the tea's tannic acid changes the color.

TAGUA NUTS

The tagua nut, which is the seed of a South American palm tree, has occasionally been used as an ivory replacement. Since the Victorian era, it has been made into jewelry and once had a prominent place in the manufacturing of buttons. Ironically, while sailors were engraving on whale

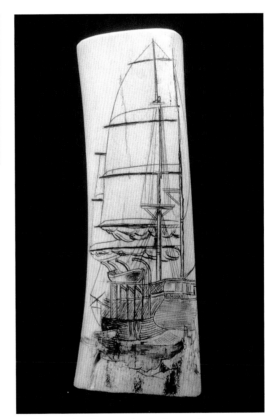

Beef bone makes for a good scrimshaw medium.

ivory, ship lore has it that this ivory substitute may have been used as ballast below decks. Today turners put it on lathes, carvers sculpt it, furniture makers use it for inlay, and scrimshanders engrave it (see Sources for Supplies).

Sometimes referred to as vegetable ivory, the tagua nut looks, feels and works much like ivory. It does have its drawbacks, however. For one, it does not grow to a large size. The nut, which tends to be slightly pointed at one end, usually ranges from 1" to 2" in diameter. Also, there may be a cavity inside the nut, or the beginnings of one indicated by cracks. Holes and cracks make it difficult to obtain a slabbed piece of any size for scrimshaw. The material also has a tendency to turn brown with age.

If you want to try tagua nuts as a substitute for ivory, bone or polymer, it is best to buy a quantity of them to experiment with. Suppliers usually offer bags of 6 to 10 nuts.

BEEF BONE

A source of scrimshaw material may be as close as the local butcher shop. Beef bone makes an ideal medium for scrimshaw art and there are no government restrictions on it. It is the shinbone that offers the best source for your needs. Despite the facts that the bone is narrow and hollow, it provides another medium for illustrations.

PREPARING THE MATERIALS

Most of the materials described above require some preparation. If you are lucky enough to have discovered a whale's tooth in great grandfather's sea chest, or someone has given you an antler and you want to try your hand at engraving it, you need to prepare the surface. You have several choices of tools: for the rough-smoothing

of a tooth, use a knife as a scraper; for faster work try a fine file. Whichever you choose, you are not aiming to remove a great deal of material. A hard substance is below the surface of the tooth that is difficult to etch. Underneath an antler's deep

Other tools are available to prepare an ivory surface, including a scraper.

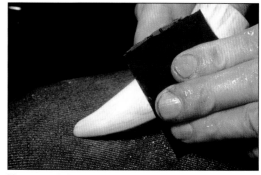

Use wet-and-dry sandpaper dampened with water to do the final smoothing on a piece of ivory.

A real whale's tooth, a form of ivory, needs to be scraped to rid the surface of ridges before engraving. Use a knife as a scraper.

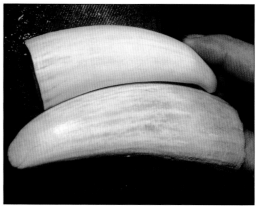

The whale's tooth on top has been scraped and sanded, while the one on the bottom has not.

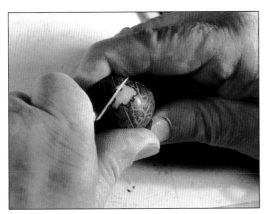

Remove the shell of the tagua nut with a knife or file.

Ivory piano keys can be scrimshawed, but the glue backing should be removed.

Secure the nut in a vise or clamp and use a saw to cut it.

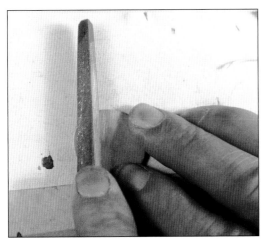

Once cut, use a file and sandpaper to smooth the revealed surface.

ridges, the material is still very dense and hard. After rough-smoothing the surface, go back and sand it. Use 220-, 320- and 400-grit wet-and-dry sandpaper with water. A note of advice: if you

want to engrave on ivory or antler, aim for marble smoothness. The smoother it is, the easier it is to engrave because the engraving tool will not be jumping between ridges and valleys.

A person with a woodworking background may be tempted to work the surface of whale or elephant ivory with a power sander. The sander is fast, but it can cause the ivory to heat up. Too much heat will crack this organic material. If you feel the need to power sand, do so cautiously with a minimum of pressure. Antler, however, is more impervious to heat.

Before working a tagua nut, remove the shell-like covering with a knife or file. Next, experiment with slabbing the nut. Do not bandsaw a nut while holding it in your fingers! Instead, secure the nut in a clamp or vise and use a handsaw. A jeweler's saw will leave a smooth surface but a coarser hacksaw will cut faster. If you slab a piece big enough to work, you will find that it engraves easily.

A piano key, smooth on its top, will have unwanted glue on the reverse side. Try soaking it in water to remove what is probably an animal glue. Once the glue is gone, the exposed surface is sanded smooth if necessary.

Beef bone, which may be the easiest scrimshaw material to find, unfortunately requires the most preparation. If it still has meat adhering to it, the bone has to be boiled, which may require hours. When the bone starts to look white, boil it again,

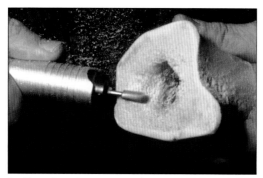

Beef bone has a honeycomb that contains marrow oil. If the honeycomb is not removed, oil in the marrow will bleed through to the surface. Use a flexible shaft tool such as the Foredom™ or Pfingst™ and a carbide cutter to remove the honeycomb.

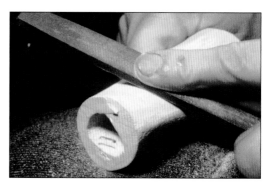

Like ivory, beef bone must have its surface prepared. If the surface is irregular, try a file for rough-smoothing.

An electric drill with a rotary cutter also removes the honeycomb.

Use a knife to scrape the surface.

this time using a solution of bleach—one pint of bleach to one gallon of water. This is a dangerous operation because it gives off a chlorine gas, which is toxic. Do the boiling outdoors. An alternative is to simply soak the cleaned bone in a solution of bleach for several days. Once the bone has a good white color to it, leave it to dry or put it into an oven at a low temperature of about 200 degrees. If the heat is too high, the bone will probably crack.

You have spent hours preparing the bone, but it is still not ready to be engraved. The next step is to remove the honeycomb material inside the bone. If this is not done, the marrow oils trapped in the honeycomb will bleed through to stain the surface. The stain will ruin the beauty of the engraving.

A grinding tool is best for removing the honeycomb. Use a flexible shaft power tool such as a Foredom™ or Pfingst™ with a carbide cutter or use a rotary cutter in an electric drill. The strength of the bone will not be undermined because enough of it is left to insure plenty of structural integrity.

One preparation remains. Like the whale's tooth, beef bone needs its surface smoothed. Use a knife, a scraper or a fine file followed up with wet-and-dry sandpaper. If you achieve a marble-smooth surface, it will actually have the look and feel of real ivory.

Beef bone is not a good material for slabbing to get thin pieces. The bone is simply too thin after the honeycomb is removed. Piano key-sized pieces would be left over. And the very act of cutting it could cause the bone to break apart. The bone itself, without altering its shape, should offer enough surface to create a piece of scrimshaw folk art. However, one end will have to

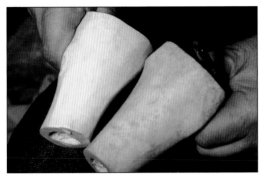

The beef bone on the left, which is the shin bone of a cow, has been prepared for engraving. The bone on the right has not been.

Use a jeweler's saw to trim away the rough ends of the beef bone.

Slabbing a beef bone results in an ivory-like surface, but there may be little to work with since the bone is thin and has a small diameter. The bone is compared to an antique cue ball that has been slabbed, a better choice for acquiring thin material.

A diamond saw makes thin slices of ivory with little waste and no dust thrown into the air. A moveable vise keeps the ivory from rotating as it is pushed into the thin blade.

be trimmed flat if you want it to stand upright. Try a jeweler's saw, not a power saw. It will make a smooth cut and waste little of the bone that you worked so hard to prepare.

Polymer ivory requires the least preparation. Its surface is already glassy smooth. If you need to cut it into smaller sizes, use a jeweler's saw or a very fine blade in a power saw to cut it and minimize waste. Use a file and wet-and-dry sandpaper to smooth rough edges.

POWER CUTTING TO SIZE

You have found a legal source of elephant ivory and have acquired a chunk of the material which may be several inches thick. It looks to be in good condition with few if any cracks or discoloration. But to put an engraving on the entire piece is a waste of precious material. Also, it will

not suit your requirements if you are making a piece of jewelry, a belt buckle, a money clip or a knife handle. The ivory has to be cut to size.

A carbide blade will cut the material quickly. But these saw blades are thick, and the resulting dust may be hazardous to your health. A steel bandsaw blade cuts ivory, but a drifting blade results in precious material being lost and the surface then has to be worked with a file and sandpaper to get rid of unwanted ridges.

The best solution for cutting ivory is a diamond saw. Motor-driven and water lubricated, the thin saw blade has diamond grit that makes short work of cutting the material. The water not only acts as a lubricant but it also absorbs the dust and prevents it from filling your workspace (see Sources for Supplies).

The diamond saw is also the ideal tool for

To cut a billiard ball, whether it is ivory or polymer, make a holding fixture out of wood, which is then clamped into the moveable vise.

Perfectly round slices of the billiard ball are left after cutting.

The diamond saw can be enclosed in a plastic box. A hole in the front of the box allows the vise to be pushed toward the blade. Some models have as an accessory a motor that power-feeds the material.

The slice of ivory or polymer may still need sanding after being cut. Use 320- to 400-grit wet-and-dry sandpaper.

slabbing a billiard ball, whether it is elephant ivory or polymer. Since you would not even think of holding the ivory sphere in your hand as you push it into a saw, you need a holding fixture. The simplest to use is one made of wood. Hollow out enough wood from a block so that half the ball fits snugly into it. Use a quick-set epoxy to hold the ball in place. Then lock the holding fixture in the saw's moveable vise. When you finish slabbing, tap the opposite side of the wood fixture with a hammer to free the ball.

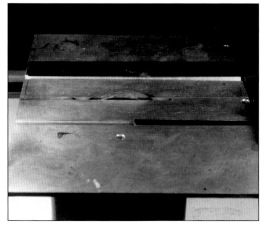

A model maker's table saw is ideal for cutting thin pieces of flat ivory or polymer.

The scrimshander of the last century most likely used a knife, sailmaker's needle or awl to engrave his tooth or bone. But a number of possibilities are available to you in the 20th century. Some tools can be homemade; others may be purchased at a home center.

Take a sewing needle, for example. It is sharp enough to engrave ivory, bone or polymer, but it is too small to handle comfortably. Find a dowel ½" in diameter and epoxy the needle into it. You now have a scrimshaw engraving tool.

An electric engraver is another useful tool. It has a reciprocating steel point that literally pounds a line into materials as hard as steel. But the power tool has its drawbacks. It is bulky to handle for long periods, and it is noisy. For special effects, however, such as a field of dots, the electric engraver quickly does the job.

THE HOBBY KNIFE

The best engraving tool for scrimshaw is as familiar to the hobbyist as paper and glue. The hobby knife, called by some manufacturers a detailing knife, has permeated the arts and crafts fields for a generation. With its metal or plastic body and interchangeable blades, it has become a simple yet effective tool for cutting a wide range of materials.

Since a variety of blades are provided with some hobby knives, make sure you use the blade with the longest bevel. If you choose an X-Acto® knife, use the number 11 blade. Before engraving with it, you need to slightly change the shape of the blade. First, break off a very small piece of the tip. The reason? It will break off eventually given the nature of the work. The hobby knife was not really designed for engraving hard materials. You

The knife is held like a pen or pencil and pulled toward the body.

The best tool for scrimshaw is a hobby knife. Remove a small piece of the tip to create a chisel-shaped end. Then put a bevel on each side of the chisel end using a small sharpening stone.

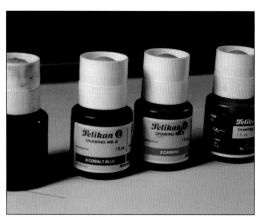

Chapter 1

Pelikan® drawing ink is one brand available for inking in engraved lines.

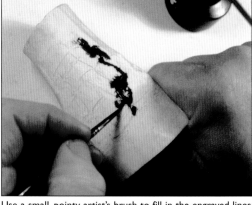

Use a small, pointy artist's brush to fill in the engraved lines with ink. Then rub the excess ink off with steel wool. The remaining ink will stay in the lines.

also need to put a bevel on each side of the new tip. Use a sharpening stone and simply rub each side of the blade end while holding the blade at a 30-degree angle to the stone. Sharpening makes the blade more like a chisel than a knife, and you will be able to turn the tool more easily as you follow curving lines.

To use the hobby knife, simply hold it as you would a pen, dig the point into the material and pull it toward you. You may at first find yourself exerting too much unnecessary pressure. Time and practice will give you the feel of how deep you really need to go into the material. Also, different effects can be achieved by how wide you engrave. This is done by making V-shaped cuts in the material, a technique that takes some practice.

THE INK

Berry juice, tobacco juice mixed with oil and lamp black were all used by the original scrimshanders to darken in their engraved lines. Waterproof and virtually indelible inks are available today. Two brands of drawing ink, which dry quickly, are commonly used: Higgens® and Pelikan®. Both offer not just the traditional black but also brown, yellow, red, green, blue and others.

The process of using ink is simple. You have engraved your lines with your knife or other etching tool. Next, apply the ink into those lines

with a small artist's brush or a cotton swab. Then rub the surface with a very fine steel wool, which comes in numbers like 000 or 0000 (3/0 or 4/0), the latter being the finest. What is left is colored engraving: black or whatever color you choose.

A FIXATIVE

Removing the excess ink from ivory and polymer is not difficult if the surface is smooth. The steel wool makes quick work of it; rubbing too hard, however, may actually take away the engraved lines if they are very shallow.

Beef bone is a problem when inking. The surface is porous and absorbs the ink. To keep from making a mess, use a fixative. Krylon® no. 1313 satin finish spray coating is readily available at hardware stores and home centers. Apply it immediately after you have penciled your pattern onto the surface. Engraving will not be affected by it since the tool easily cuts through the coating. Applying the fixative makes ink removal, even on non-porous materials like ivory and polymer, much easier.

DEALING WITH MISTAKES

Unless you are a professional engraver or a talented artist, it is likely you will make mistakes. The knife slips and a groove is created beyond the pencil line. Or, an engraved line ends up where it does not belong. Several possibilities are open.

These include scraping off the etched line, which takes some skill so that little of the engraving is lost. Another is covering the mistake with tape or a wax to keep the ink from running into the line. Of course you can begin again using a new piece or scrape away all of the engraved lines. Starting over should be based on how much time you have into the piece and the availability or scarcity of the material.

Some scrimshanders coat the surface with ink, and then make their engraved lines. White lines appear on a dark background. Scratchboard, which is a board that has a thin coating of plaster painted black, looks similar. When it is scratched, the white plaster shows through. Etching through a black background is an acceptable technique if you are skilled enough to work without a pattern.

On the other hand, if you are using the scribe-first-and-ink-second method, can you be sure you have gone over all the pencil lines of the pattern? You might think you are finished engraving, only to discover after rubbing off the excess ink that you missed some important lines. Not only that, but you have also removed the pencil lines when you rubbed off the ink.

The obvious difficulty of working a white surface is that it is hard to keep track of the lines. A good light source is the best solution. A fluorescent light directly over the work effectively illuminates the surface and allows the engraved lines to show up. You may have to tilt the piece to catch the reflections of the lines, but they will appear.

MAGNIFICATION

Most scrimshaw involves small pieces with fine detail. Even if you are working on something as big as a moose antler, you need to magnify the fine lines of engraving to prevent eye strain. Two tools are useful for magnification. One is a vision visor, an optical glass lens with an adjustable headband. The price for the visor is usually in the ten-dollar range. The other is a magnifier lamp. More costly than a vision visor, the lamp uses a

When engraving small pieces, use a vision visor as pictured or a magnifier lamp.

circular bulb and a magnification lens. In addition, the arms, under spring tension, allow the lamp to be moved into almost any position.

PATTERN SOURCES

Literally every magazine and illustrated book offers the possibility of a pattern. If your themes are nautical, a wide array of books on sailing ships can be found in libraries and bookstores. If your interest is in animals, again look to books and clipart for your sources.

Copy machines, almost universally available, will reduce the size of the picture and make it fit onto something as small as a bolo or a piece of jewelry.

TRANSFERRING PATTERNS

Most of us are familiar with tracing paper. The material looks white but is nearly transparent when it is placed over a drawing. Acetate paper is a good substitute for standard tracing paper. Thicker and stronger, it offers a very clear view of the subject being traced. Use a paint marker because pencil and regular ink will not adhere to its surface.

The advantage of the acetate paper is that you can easily copy a picture or illustration without having to press down hard on a book or magazine page. Too much pressure leaves unsightly impressions on the paper.

The next step is getting the copied drawing onto the scrimshaw material. A transfer paper called carbonless paper has been on the market for some time. It is gray instead of blue-black and does not leave your fingertips looking as if they have been to the police station. Graphite paper is also available, which leaves what looks like a pencil line that is erasable. Still another paper is a white carbon, which is particularly useful when transferring patterns onto a dark surface.

Patterns for scrimshaw work are virtually everywhere. This ship illustration was taken from an auction gallery catalog.

Note: In the following photos, the ship pattern will show you how to apply a pattern to a rounded surface, while the sailor pattern will show you the methods for flat surfaces.

Use a piece of clear plastic or acetate paper to trace a pattern.

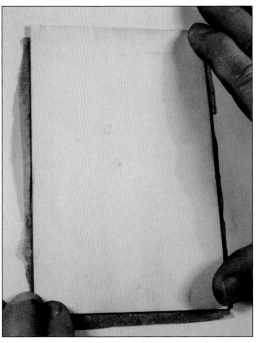

Finding a piece of material the right dimensions for the pattern is obviously important. Pictured is a slab of elephant ivory.

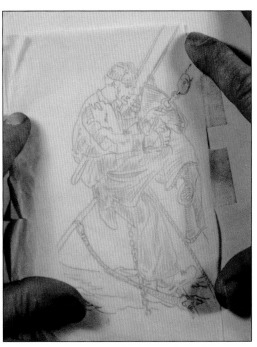

A pattern is drawn up to fit the ivory and traced.

Put a piece of carbon paper or the transfer paper of your choice between the pattern and material. Use clear tape to hold the pattern to the material. Here, carbon paper was chosen.

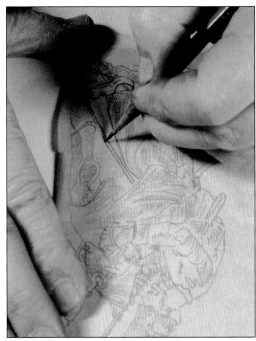

Use a hard lead pencil and draw over the pattern.

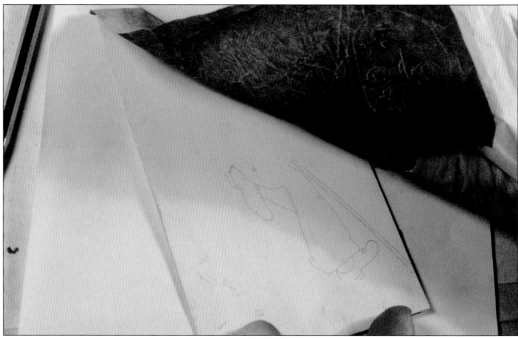

Lift up the pattern and carbon to check on the progress. Make sure the pattern stays taped in place. It has to be in the same position after it is put back down on the medium.

Irregularly shaped objects such as beef bone require more care in positioning the pattern.

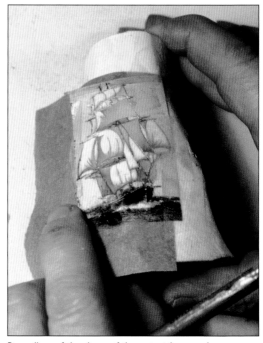

Regardless of the shape of the material, use carbon paper, graphite paper, or the transfer paper of your choice to transfer the pattern. Here, again, carbon paper was chosen.

Draw over the pattern so that the carbon paper leaves an impression.

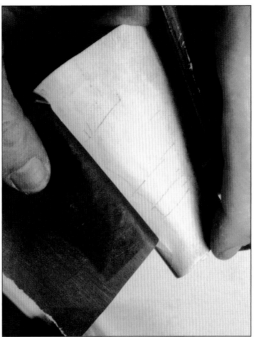

Check frequently on how the material is picking up the lines left by the carbon paper.

TRANSFERRING A PATTERN WITH TAPE

There should be no problem making a transfer onto a flat surface. But what if you have a whale tooth or an antler to work on? How do you transfer the pattern onto a small and rounded surface?

A trick to working that impossible surface is to use clear or "invisible" masking tape. Pencil the pattern onto tracing paper; then lay the tape over it with just enough pressure so that the tape will pick up the carbon while not permanently sticking to the paper. You may need to join several pieces of tape since a single piece is relatively narrow. Once the pattern has been transferred to the tape, you simply adhere it to the surface to be scrimshawed. There will be small folds in the tape because it will not perfectly cover an irregular surface. Simply cut through the folds and overlap the ends. Redraw and reconnect the lines that got cut away or separated. To engrave the surface simply cut

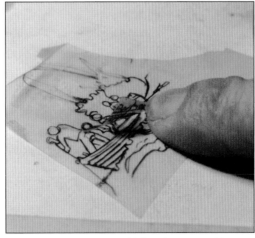

Take pieces of clear or "invisible" masking tape and lay them over the pattern as it appears on the tracing paper. If the tape is carefully lifted it will bring away some of the pencil carbon.

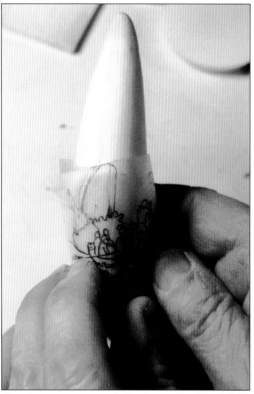

Place the tape over a rounded surface such as this whale's tooth.

The tape and pattern are in place.

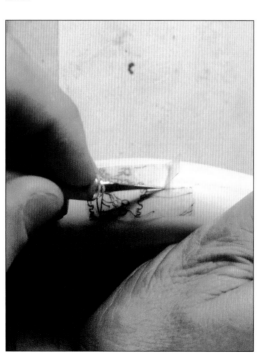

Engrave through the tape. Although it will shred, the engraved lines will remain on the material.

through the tape. If it starts to shred and tear away, discard pieces so long as you have completed the engraving underneath.

If you have difficulty removing the tape, try rubbing it off with mineral spirits and a paper towel. If more abrasion is needed, use 4/0 steel wool.

A HARD PENCIL

It is always best to work with a hard pencil. A 2H is ideal for transferring patterns and drawing on the surface to be scrimshawed. Try sharpening the point on an emery board or a piece of sandpaper. The point will be stubby but it will not readily break as you bear down on it.

KEEPING IT SIMPLE

One of the secrets of making scrimshaw work easier is keeping the basic pattern simple at first and building up the details in stages. If you are doing a sailing ship, for example, do not transfer all of the details to the scrimshaw pattern.

Outline just the ship, the masts, and the sails. Save the fine detail such as rigging for later.

Establish the basic outline, engrave, ink the surface, and rub off the excess. Go back and draw in the rigging, hull details, water and clouds.

Each feature takes a separate inking. Be careful not to rub out the engraved lines with the steel wool. Techniques and tips for shading and coloring are discussed in the next chapter.

Keep the pencil sharp using an emery board.

Try wet-and-dry sandpaper to sharpen the pencil point. It is not necessary to have a long, thin point that will easily break.

Not all of the details of this ship should be done right away. Start with the simple outline of the sails and hull.

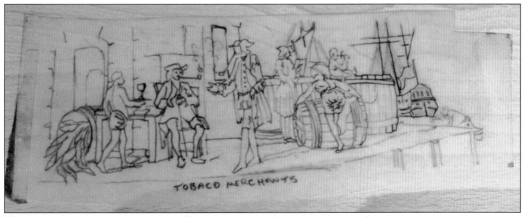

There is a lot going on in this illustration of early tobacco merchants, so engraving is done in stages. Note that there is no shading on the illustration. It is done last and mostly by eye.

Chapter 3

COPYRIGHT

A legal note of importance: although many illustrations and photographs are available to the amateur scrimshander, be aware that most will be copyrighted. Copyright means that they may not be reproduced without permission of the copyright owner if you intend to sell your work.

Although there are artists who are unscrupulous enough to copy without giving credit, you might consider how you would feel having your work appear under someone else's name in a major gallery or shop. It is necessary to obtain written permission from the owner or use material for which the copyright has expired.

Lines missed in the first stage of pattern transfer are drawn in.

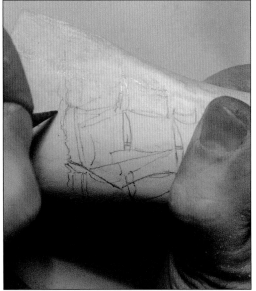

Details such as water can be added if they do not complicate the pattern early on. Doing the engraving in stages prevents mistakes of putting lines in where they do not belong.

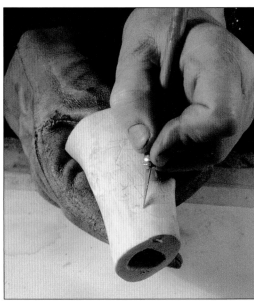

Working on a small, irregularly shaped object that cannot lie flat requires hand protection. Wear a heavy work glove or a Kevlar® glove.

When shading your illustrations to create the illusion of depth, roundness and shadow, study the principles of pen and ink drawing. The principal technique is the use of parallel lines. These are called hatching. When hatching, lines are usually broken or interrupted, meaning that they look like the dashes of Morse code. Cross-hatching, meaning that lines intersect or cross over each other, is used for areas with lots of shadow or complex textures. Trees in a forest can be illustrated with cross-hatched lines.

A readily available example of cross-hatching is in your wallet or purse. Look closely at a piece of paper currency and notice that shading and shadows are done not with brushstrokes but instead with hatched and cross-hatched lines.

A few early scrimshanders created their illustrations using dots rather than lines. They would lay an illustration over the tooth or bone and poke through the paper with a pointed steel tool. The technique is called stippling. Shading and shadows are also be done by stippling. The closer and tighter the patterns of dots, the more shade or shadow is created. Widely spaced dots give an open look. Try using a needle or a sharply pointed awl. Stippling may not be the best technique for a beginning scrimshander, but, when perfected, the results are striking.

TIPS

An excellent book for the beginner is *Pen & Ink Techniques*, by Frank Lohan (see Bibliography). Lohan takes the reader from the basics of paper and pens to simple projects such as walls and fences to panoramas and landscapes. Many of his patterns are excellent for scrimshaw work.

If you are interested in creating scrimshaw with nautical themes, try shading. You might desire to do nothing more than an outline of a sailing ship, but soon realize that it would look better with some depth and contrast. Start by darkening in the hull with horizontal or vertical lines. Next, give the sails a feeling of billowing motion by following the contours of the sails with hatched lines. Curving the lines will create the illusion of roundness. Next try adding a cloud or two

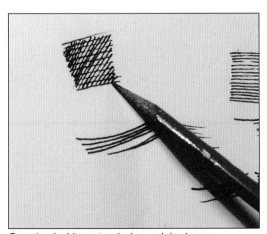

Cross-hatched lines give shadow and depth to an illustration.

Hatching can consist simply of parallel lines. Bringing them closer together darkens an area. Farther apart lightens an area.

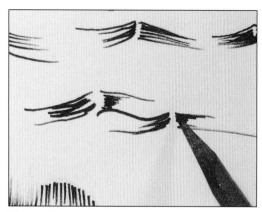

Chapter 6

Waves and water are defined with curving, parallel lines.

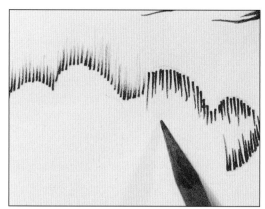

Clouds are represented with series of parallel lines of differing lengths.

behind the sailing ship. Then add short, vertically hatched lines coming off the curves. Almost immediately the clouds start to show some depth instead of flatness.

Shading should not be done too early. Establish the basic shapes first. If you try to engrave all of the details at once, they will likely look muddled.

Micro carving tools are useful. To create a porthole, use a tiny gouge and lift out a small circle or square of material. The ink will fill in the tiny hole and create a dark portal. Or, use a fine drill to bore in a round porthole or other small opening.

COLORING

The beauty of scrimshaw art often comes with coloring. Animals are given their natural colors, water is made blue, and sunsets are enhanced with reds and yellows. With the exception of beef bone, coloring has to be accomplished with lines. Do the outline in black ink; when you add new lines, simply apply a different color to them. To create water, for example, use a variety of hatched and cross-hatched lines. Then apply blue ink.

Beef bone offers interesting possibilities. Because the surface is porous, it acts much like a canvas. Inks are applied without having to engrave series of lines to pick up the colors. The problem, however, is controlling the ink and keeping it from running into areas where it does not belong. The best solution is to use the spray fixative Krylon® no. 1313 satin finish. Spray the

Clouds are also done with simple semi-circles. Birds are drawn with only a few lines.

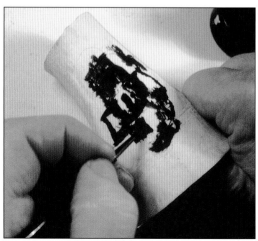

First, ink the engraving. Because beef bone is porous, it is colored more easily than other materials.

entire bone; then carefully scrape away an area where you want to apply color. If the ink should flow where it is not wanted, it too can be scraped away. If you can master the flow of ink, the effect can be pleasing and worth the effort, especially since beef bone costs so little.

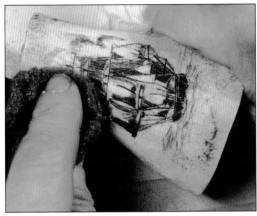
Then, remove excess ink with steel wool.

Use the bone as if it were a palette and color the surface.

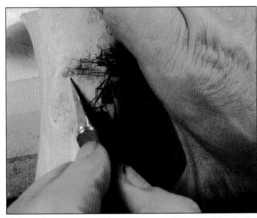
If the color goes out of bounds, scrape it away with a knife.

Try inking different areas to enhance the scrimshaw.

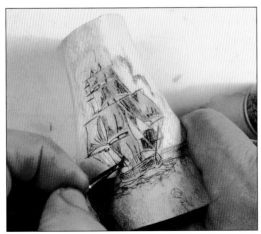
Hatched lines are inked to add shading.

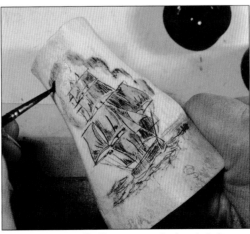
Inks such as Pelikan® offer a variety of colors, including blues, greens, reds, yellows and others.

1 Find a suitable illustration or picture for scrimshawing. The ship is a painting that was reproduced in an auction gallery catalog.

2 Position the tracing paper over the picture. Make sure both are securely held on a flat surface with tape.

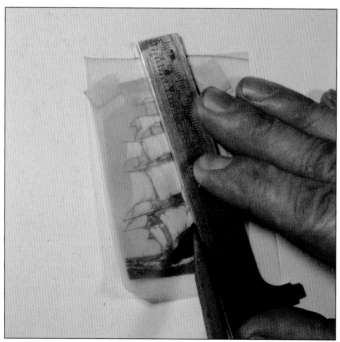

3 Use a straight edge to trace straight lines.

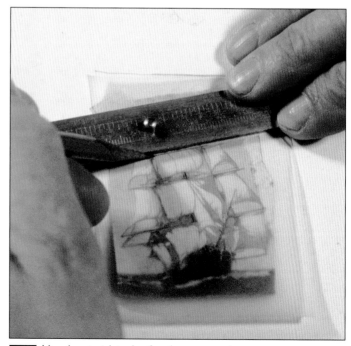

4 Use the straight edge for the spars and masts.

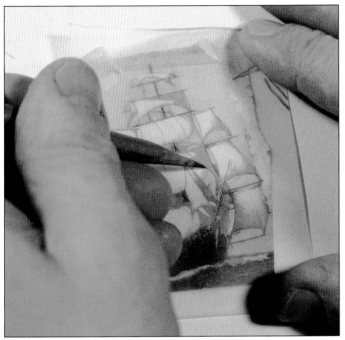

5 Freehand the contours of the sails.

6 Outline the hull and waterline.

7 Take the tracing paper and place it over the scrimshaw material, in this case a piece of elephant ivory. Keep the picture nearby for reference. Note that not every detail of the ship has been transferred.

8 Place carbon paper between the material and the tracing paper.

Chapter 1

THE PROJECT

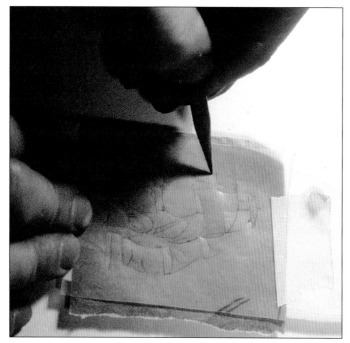

9 Begin tracing.

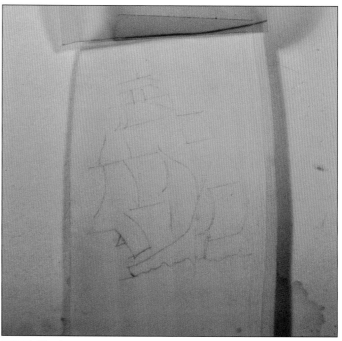

10 Check on the progress by noting how the lines are being transferred to the scrimshaw material.

11 After drawing the lines, apply a fixative such as Krylon® no. 1303 or no. 1313 spray coating.

12 Note the difference between the area coated with the Krylon® finish and the area at the top that is not.

13 Before engraving, make sure the material, if flat, is held firmly to the work surface. Use a piece of tape if necessary.

14 Engraving begins with the straight lines.

15 Engrave the curved lines of the sails.

16 Once the basic outline has been completed, engrave parallel lines on the hull to give it definition.

THE PROJECT

17 Engraving after the first stage.

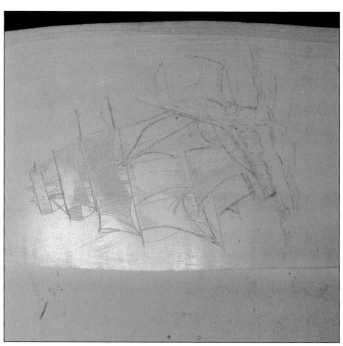

18 Engraving completed with a variety of hatched and cross-hatched lines to give shadow and depth.

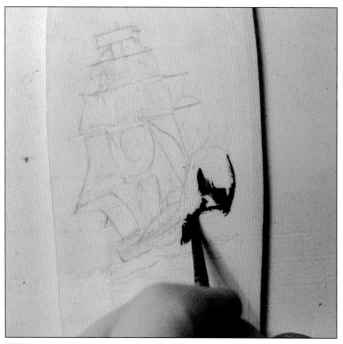

19 Use a dark ink and an artist's brush to color the engraved lines.

20 It is not necessary to coat the entire piece of scrimshaw with ink.

21 Work the brush into the engraved lines.

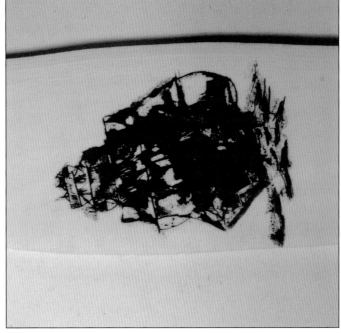

22 Inking complete.

23 Rub off excess ink with a fine steel wool such as a 3/0 or a 4/0.

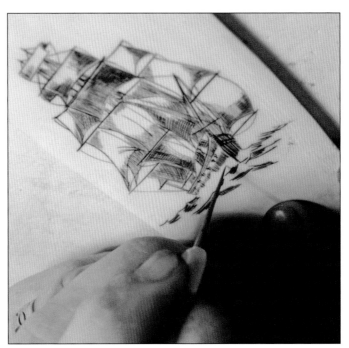

24 Use a pointed steel tool to put into the material a series of dots to represent spray.

THE PROJECT

25 Cover the dots with ink.

26 Remove the excess ink to reveal the stippled effect.

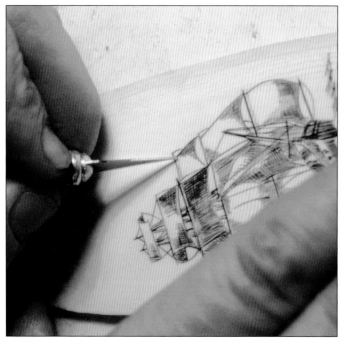

27 Put into the upper sails a series of hatched or parallel lines that will pick up a new color.

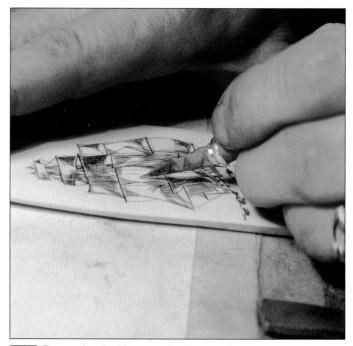

28 Engrave hatched lines on the lower sails.

29 Rinse the brush before applying a new color.

30 Apply a yellow ink.

31 Confine the ink to the hatched lines.

32 Rub off the excess ink with steel wool.

THE PROJECT

33 More lines in the wake of the ship enhance the illustration.

34 Apply color to the engraved lines.

35 New colors are added to the sails by engraving more lines.

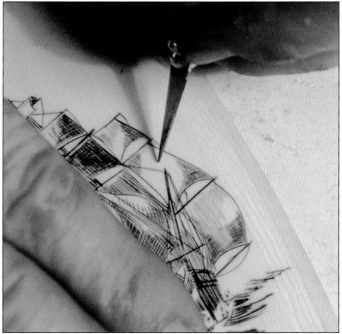

36 There is no limit to how much color you can put into a piece when using the hatching technique.

37 Apply the fixative between successive engravings to keep the colors from running into each other.

38 Each time color is applied, rub off the excess ink.

39 Finished! The water is colored blue. Try thinning the ink with water and use it diluted to vary the color.

Chapter 8

Fakes, Preservation and Museums

GENUINE OR FAKE?

You have been snooping around antique shops and shows, and you come across a scrimshawed whale's tooth. The dealer assures you it is a genuine piece, and the price tag would seem to bear that out. You want to purchase it and admire what a scrimshander of the past created. To buy or not to buy?

Unfortunately, it is difficult to tell the antique from the fake. But there are some on-site inspections and tests you can try to give you a better idea of the authenticity of the piece. If you have a scrap of flannel or silk available, rub the tooth with it briskly. A polymer tooth will pick of small pieces of paper because of a static charge. A real tooth will neutralize that charge. However, the imitation may have been treated with an anti-static chemical.

Another tip: find a magnifying glass and give the piece a close inspection. Look for fine cracks that come with age. Also look at the cavity end of the tooth and check for grain lines. Reproductions often have simulated cracks, but polymer has no grain.

Ultraviolet light and X-rays are also used to root out the fakes, but these are not practical for most of us looking to buy a genuine piece of scrimshaw. The melt test is the one seemingly foolproof method of determining whether the scrimshaw piece, be it a whale's tooth, bone, elephant ivory, fossil ivory or walrus tusk, is genuine. Take a heated needle, find an inconspicuous place on the piece, and insert it. Polymer will melt. Bone and ivory may smoke a bit, but that is all that will happen.

Another option is having an appraiser familiar with scrimshaw check the piece out. If this is possible, you may be saving yourself quite a bit of money or making a good investment since genuine scrimshaw often sells in the thousands and doesn't seem to decrease in value.

Pictured is a tooth made from synthetic ivory. Often sold as originals, such reproductions usually have very detailed engravings of ships.

Compare the imitation ivory on the left with a genuine sperm whale's tooth on the right.

When trying to determine whether a scrimshawed tooth is genuine, check the cavity for grain lines.

Houses that dry out in the winter can be a problem. Homes in arid lands will also cause problems for ivory. Thinly slabbed ivory will warp. Keeping the humidity stable with a humidifier or even a dish of water is the best answer to preserving scrimshaw. Polymer on the other hand is extremely stable and will suffer little with temperature and humidity changes.

Does scrimshaw need to be cleaned? A genuine piece of ivory should never be treated with any solvent or detergent. The risk of removing the coloring agents is just too great. This holds true for your own piece. India ink is not impervious to many cleaners.

PRESERVING YOUR SCRIMSHAW

Very little maintenance is needed with scrimshaw, but some precautions are suggested. Real ivory likes an environment with mild humidity. It does not like extremes in cold and heat. Too much temperature change will crack the material.

A TRIP TO A MUSEUM

To get a first-hand idea of what real scrimshaw looks like, take a trip to a maritime museum. A good collection is housed at the Mystic Seaport Museum in Mystic, Connecticut. Call first for hours open and schedules of special events.

P atterns are ubiquitous. They are as near at hand as the closest illustration or photograph, although it may be necessary to trace, reduce or do some freehand work to customize them for a particular project.

The patterns that follow—original pen and ink drawings by Al Jetter—provide an edge. His sailboats, sea birds, seascapes and shells and other drawings offer pleasing projects for the novice scrimshander. The illustrations also indicate where to add highlights and shadows. The patterns need not be engraved in their entirety. For example, isolate a seagull or boat and leave out the background. With scrimshaw, the scope of the project is limited only by the size of the medium.

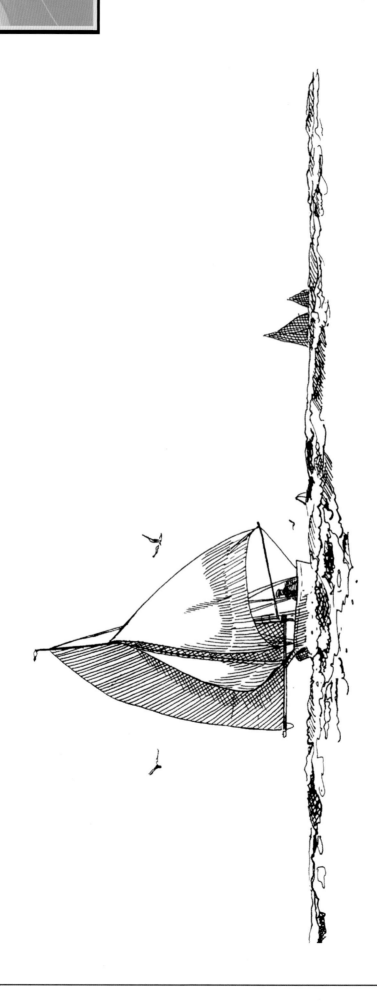

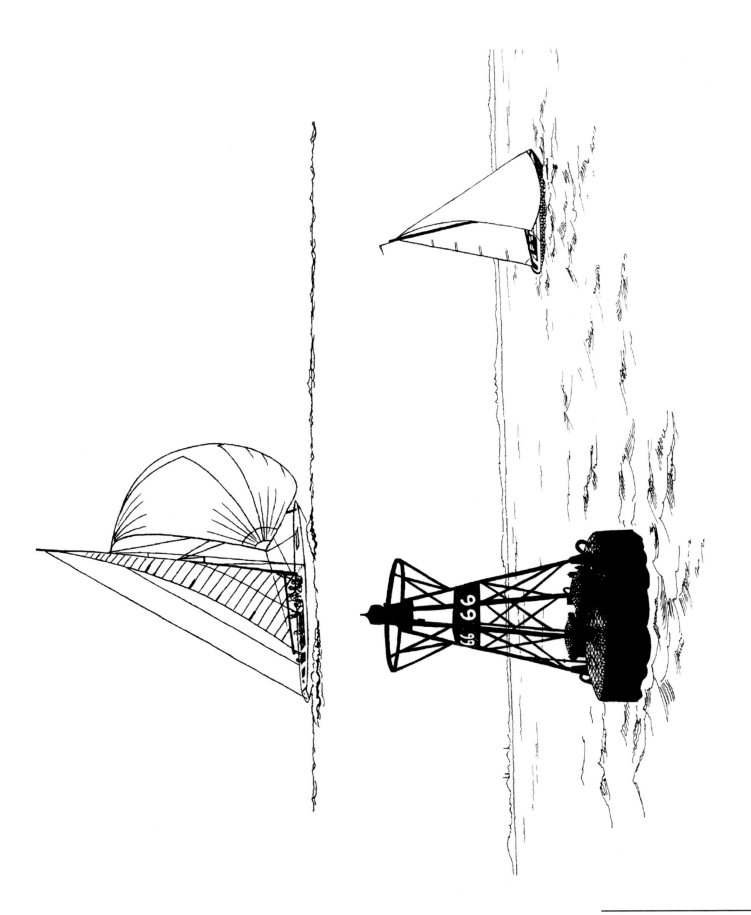

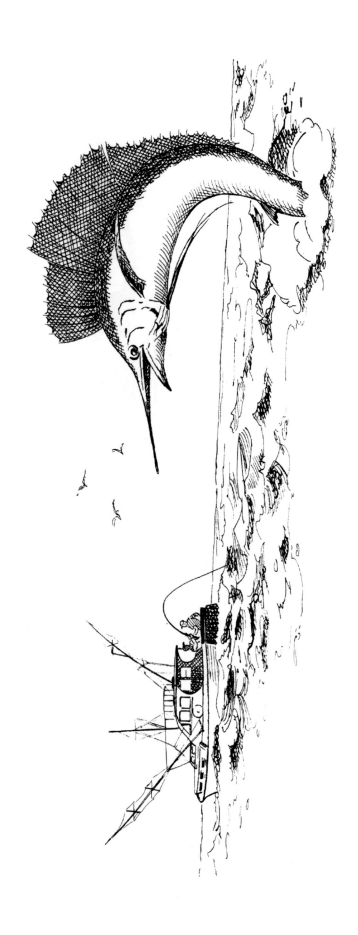

Chapter 9

Books About Scrimshaw

Barnes, Clare
John F. Kennedy, Scrimshaw Collector
Boston, MA. Little, Brown and Company, 1964.

Carpenter, Charles H., Jr. And Mary Grace Carpenter
The Decorative Arts and Crafts of Nantucket
New York, NY. Dodd Mead & Co., in cooperation with the Nantucket Historical Association et al., 1987.

Chapelle, Howard I.
The History of American Sailing Ships
New York, NY. W.W. Norton & Company, Inc., 1935.

Flayderman, E. Norman
Scrimshaw and Scrimshanders, Whales and Fishermen.
New Milford, CT. N. Flayderman & Co., 1972.

Gilkerson, William
The Scrimshander: The Nautical Ivory Worker and His Art of Scrimshaw, Historical and Contemporary
San Francisco, CA. Troubador Press, 1975.

Hellman, Nina, and Norman Brouwer
A Mariner's Fancy: The Whaleman's Art of Scrimshaw
New York, NY. South Street Seaport and Balsam Press, 1992.

Linsley, Leslie
Scrimshaw, A traditional folk art, A contemporary craft
New York, NY. Hawthorne Books. 1976.

Malley, Richard C.
"Graven by the fishermen themselves": Scrimshaw in Mystic Seaport Museum
Mystic, CT. Mystic Seaport Museum, 1983.

McManus, Michael
A Treasury of American Scrimshaw
New York, NY. Penguin Studio, 1997.

Meyer, Charles R.
Whaling and the Art of Scrimshaw
New York, NY. David McKay Company, Inc., 1976.

Stackpole, Edouard A.
Scrimshaw at Mystic Seaport
Mystic, CT. The Mariner Historical Association, 1958.

Nautical History and Illustrations

Ashley, Clifford W.
The Yankee Whaler
Garden City, NY. Dover Publications, 1991.

Cooke, Edward William
Sailing Vessels in Authentic Early Nineteenth-Century Illustrations
Garden City, NY. Dover Publications, 1989.

Grafton, Carol Berlanger (ed.)
Ready-to-Use Old-Fashioned Nautical Illustrations
Mineola, NY. Dover Publications, Inc. 1991.

Spence, Bill
Harpooned: The Story of Whaling
New York, NY. Crescent Books, 1980.

Whipple, A.B.C.
The Whalers
Alexandria, VA. Time-Life Books, 1979.

Pen and Ink

Lohan, Frank
Pen and Ink Techniques
Chicago, IL. Contemporary Books, 1978.

Lohan, Frank
Pen and Ink Themes
Chicago, IL. Contemporary Books, 1981.

Engraving

Meek, James B.
The Art of Engraving
Montezuma, IA. F. Brownell & Son, Publishers, 1973.

Authors' Note: Some of the books are out of print. Try your library system or a book search service such as **www.amazon.com** or **www.barnesandnoble.com**.

Magazines of Interest

Blade
Krause Publications
700 E. State St.
Iola, WI 54990-0001
715-445-2214

Sea History
National Maritime Historical Society
PO Box 68
Peekskill, NY 10566
1-800-221-NMHS

Directory of Featured Artists

Kristen Barndt
kris@kabstudio.com
www.KABstudio.com

Deb Donnelly
1668 C Willamsburg Court
Wheaton, IL 60187
(630) 730-8809
www.print2paint.com

Bob Hergert
12 Geer Circle
Port Orford, OR 97465
(541) 332-3010
hergert@scrimshander.com
www.scrimshander.com

Anouk Johanna
PO Box 2036
Santa Cruz, CA 95063
(831) 338-7716
anook@msn.com
www.wearablebears.com

Catherine Nerbonne
PO Box 662
Jennison, MI 49429
(616) 532-6994
nerbonne@aol.com
www.scrimshaw.net

Steve Paszkiewicz
c/o Fox Chapel Publishing
1970 Broad Street
East Petersburg, PA 17520
(717) 560-4703

Viveca Sahlin
viveca@scrimart.u.se
www.scrimart.u.se

Kurt Sperry
kurt@fineartscrimshaw.com
www.fineartscrimshaw.com

Mark Thogerson
PO Box 882
Muskegon, MI 49443
mark@scrimshaw.net
www.scrimshaw.net

Diamond Saws

Kingsley North Inc.
910 Brown St.
PO Box 216
Norway, MI 49870
906-563-9228
www.kingsleynorth.com

Rio Grande
6901 Washington NE
Albuquerque, NM 87109
1-800-545-6566
www.riogrande.com

Legal Ivory and Scrimshaw Supplies

The Boone Trading Company, Inc.
PO Box 669
562 Coyote Road
Brinnon, WA 98320
1-800-423-1945
www.boonetrading.com

African Import Co.
Alan Zanotti
20 Braunecker Rd.
Plymouth, MA 02360
508-746-8552

Alternative Ivory

GPS Agencies
Units 3 and 3A
Hambrook Business Centre
Cheesemans Lane
Hambrook
West Sussex England PO18 8XP
01243-574444
www.gpsagencies.co.uk

Tagua Nuts

Christian J. Hummul Co.
PO Box 522
Nescopeck, PA 18635-0522
1-800-762-0235
www.craftwoods.com

Treeline
1221 East 1120 South
Provo, Utah 84606
1-800-598-2743
www.treelineusa.com

Woodcraft
PO Box 1686
Parkersburg, WV 26102-1686
1-800-225-1153
www.woodcraft.com

Micro Carving Tools

Woodcraft
PO Box 1686
Parkersburg, WV 26102-1686
1-800-225-1153
www.woodcraft.com

Other sources for wood carving tools and supplies can be found in the pages of the quarterly *Wood Carving Illustrated*, available on newsstands or from the publisher.
Wood Carving Illustrated
1970 Broad St.
East Petersburg, PA 17520
1-800-457-9112

Mystic Seaport—The Museum of America and the Sea

75 Greenmanville Avenue
PO Box 6000
Mystic, CT 06355-0990
Visitor Information: (860) 572-5315 or
1-888-9SEAPORT (1-888-973-2767)
Administration: (860) 572-0711
www.mysticseaport.org

The Maritime Gallery at Mystic Seaport
PO Box 6000
47 Greenmanville Avenue
Mystic, CT 06355
(860) 572-5388
Fax: (860) 572-5324
gallery@mysticseaport.org
www.mysticseaport.org/gallery